LOVE IN THE GARDENS OF MACANTAR

LOVE IN THE GARDENS OF MACANTAR

A Spiritual Journey of Healing from Codependency and Relationship Addiction

Revised Edition

LISA ACOR LAUREL

iUniverse LLC
Bloomington

Love in the Gardens of Macantar
A Spiritual Journey of Healing from Codependency and Relationship Addiction

iUniverse books may be ordered through booksellers or by contacting:

iUniverse LLC
1663 Liberty Drive
Bloomington, IN 47403
www.iuniverse.com
1-800-Authors (1-800-288-4677)

Because of the dynamic nature of the Internet, any web addresses or links contained in this book may have changed since publication and may no longer be valid. The views expressed in this work are solely those of the author and do not necessarily reflect the views of the publisher, and the publisher hereby disclaims any responsibility for them.

Any people depicted in stock imagery provided by Thinkstock are models, and such images are being used for illustrative purposes only.

Certain stock imagery © Thinkstock.

ISBN: 978-1-4620-1317-3 (sc)
ISBN: 978-1-4620-1318-0 (ebk)

Printed in the United States of America

iUniverse rev. date: 07/01/2013

Contents

Foreword.. ix
Introduction... xi

PART I: *THE END*

Somewhere In The Mix Of Things.. 3
The Last Night... 4
The 1st Day 5
The 2nd Day 7
The 3rd Day.. 8
The 4th Day.. 9
The 5th Day.. 10
The 6th Day.. 11
The 7th Through The 11th Day 12
The 12th Day.. 13
The 13th Day.. 15
The 16th Day.. 17
The 17th Day.. 18
The 18th To The 24th Day.. 19
The 25th Day.. 20
The 44th Day.. 22
The 50th Day.. 24
The 58th Day.. 25
The 60th Day.. 27
The 62nd Day 29
The 65th Day.. 31
The 71st Day 32
The 72nd Day 33

PART II: *THE IN-BETWEEN*

The King of the Butterflies.. 37
The 75th Day.. 38
The 80th Day.. 40
The 85th Day.. 41

The 94th Day..42

The 112th Day..45

The 154th Day..46

The 168th Day..48

The 169th Day..49

PART III: *THE BEGINNING*

In The Lines Of The Labyrinth 53

The 186th Day..54

The 187th Day..56

The 230th Day..57

The 245th Day..59

The 260th Day..60

The 265th Day..61

The 276th Day..62

The 290th Day..63

The 310th Day..65

The 319th Day..66

The 336th Day..67

The 337th Day..68

The 339th Day..69

The 342nd Day...70

The 345th Day..71

The 351st Day...73

The 353rd Day..74

The 356th Day..75

The 365th Day..76

Afterword Revised 81

Bibliography...85

This book is dedicated to my child
with all my Hope and Love.

FOREWORD

This revision has been undertaken for a variety of reasons. The largest reason is because of my self-imposed deadline, the editing was definitely lacking. The praise and criticism of Macantar was taken into careful consideration. The suggestion that mainly stood out was to introduce the definition of Macantar in the beginning of the story. I'd like to take this opportunity to clarify that it has taken me my whole life to finally appreciate the meaning of the word Macantar. If the reader will sit with the story, and then read the definition in the end, the meaning of the word will hopefully become heartfelt, and will eventually integrate as a part of our core. Living in the mystery of life, and the unknown is part of acceptance and growing up. It is the foundation for building faith with our Creator.

In the first version of the book, the characters were only a vague sketch, as I wanted the reader to not compare, but to identify with the players of their own experiences rather than my experience. However, I have been asked to be more defined. Two years following the release of the first edition, I had learned some hard lessons about my idealism. I have clarified this in the Afterword of this revision.

The first edition was the cake without the icing or the cherry. Hope you will enjoy the Macantar journey, dear readers . . . including the icing on the spoon!

Lisa Acor Laurel

INTRODUCTION

In all of life's usual battles and the specific consequences I have experienced from my addiction to substances, along with my underlying codependent behavior, the hardest challenge was to finally let go a relationship that I thought was my lifeline. Because of my codependence, which is rooted in childhood events leading me to think other people's feelings and needs are more important than my own, I was dying in unfulfilling and sometimes dangerous relationships. If I were to survive, I needed to feel the fear of leaving and do it anyway.

Being with my husband for many years in a textbook abusive relationship, I began using alcohol to take the edge off, and escalated into alcoholic drinking. After I divorced my husband, I found myself in another relationship that was just as abusive. During that new relationship, I was able to somehow regain my sobriety, and began to understand the damaging dynamics. Reading every book on relationships I could get my hands on, and twisting myself into a pretzel to "make this work", eventually the emotional pain became too much to bear. If no action was taken to save myself, I feared a return to drinking would be the result, or worse.

Fortunately, I was able to prepare before taking steps to walk away. My relationship with my Higher Power was intact, and I had worked hard at becoming financially stable. However, not everyone has the opportunity to prepare. Sometimes the rug of life is pulled out from under us: an affair may be uncovered, the spouse may be violent, or one partner may force the other out. Whether prepared to leave or not, the fear can be the same. Fear of the unknown can be more terrifying than what we do know. The temporary bandages provided by shopping, drinking, affairs, over-working, over-sleeping, or any other self-destructive behavior will soon make matters worse. The pain I may face on my freedom journey could not possibly be as bad as the pain I was facing in the relationship.

Leaving a relationship may not be the answer for everyone. However, for those who have exhausted all other options and finally closing the door on a relationship may be the only choice for sanity. It is our right to give ourselves the time and commitment that we were willing to give everyone else. There are many books, therapies, and support groups to help along the way.

The following journal entries reflect my movement from a state of self-pity and blaming others to taking responsibility for my own happiness and fulfillment.

> May the road rise up to meet you.
> May the wind always be at your back.
> May the sunshine be warm upon your face.
> May the rain fall soft upon your fields.
> And until we meet again,
> May God hold you in the palm of His hand.
>
> —Old Irish prayer

PART I

THE END

SOMEWHERE IN THE MIX OF THINGS

In the Black of the Night and the softness of the rain
I fall down to the ground, defeated.
In the silence; I feel cut open.
My Creator knows my Pain.
I am back at the beginning of Time.
There is no Thinking.
There is no Breath.

My Defenses are worn to the bone.
Like a Broken baby bird, I need my mother's wings to protect me.
My heart makes no sound.
I need mending.

Gently . . . . slowly . . . .
Very slowly . . . .

Through the Broken shards of beliefs held dear,
I am shown the way back to Love.

THE LAST NIGHT

This is the last night before Seth leaves for India and will be gone for two months. This is my chance to break free. He may know this is coming, or he may not. I have had my last lash of abuse. No more sleepless nights, or too much sleeping, or feeling guilt, anxiety, anguish, disgust, rage, self-loathing, him-loathing, loneliness, fear, hope he'll change, hope I'll change, hope God will intervene, suicidal thoughts, homicidal thoughts. No more thinking, *Will he call? Should I call? Who can I talk to? Who will listen? Who will understand?* No more feeling confused, embarrassed, ashamed, frustrated, unfocused, sick, jealous, suspicious, insecure, inadequate, angry with everyone, angry at myself, angry with him, angry with God.

This is the last night. A friend sent me a poem that spoke of healing. It came at the right time.

I consulted the ancient Rune stones. They said the Universe supports my decision.

I opened the Bible, and a phrase caught my eye: "Why are you wasting this precious oil on his head?"

This is the time. The veil has parted. I must walk through or be forever lost in a cycle of harsh negativity.

I will smell his body's scent tonight for the last time as he sits near me—the scent that always pulls me back to him with a mother's maternal feeling, the need to protect him like he is a child, and not a grown man.

After tonight, my heart won't leap, and my stomach won't churn over every time I hear a car in the driveway. My phone won't ring with his number. Oh, a pang of reminiscence—or is it fear or guilt? I need a rest. No more.

THE 1ST DAY

While driving Seth to the hunters lodge, the drop-off point to meet his friend Horace for a ride the rest of the way to the airport, he screamed and intimidated. His blonde hair seems to be taking on a jaundice-yellow color as it is now contrasted against his rage-red face. His perfect rows of white teeth now appear as menacing fangs. As he arches up over me from the passenger side, it seems as if he is growing bigger. His blue eyes were now more of a blue-black; as unfeeling as a set of blouse buttons. I couldn't absorb his words. They seemed to deflect off an invisible shield that surrounds my body. I certainly would be justified in stopping my vehicle and letting him out right here at the bank's drive through window, but then I would never be sure that he got on the plane and left for India. Gripping the wheel, I keep driving and do not respond. What set off his rage I hadn't a clue. I have never been sure about what set him off, and I could not find a way to stop the rage once it started.

Finally, arriving at the lodge, I suggest I walk him into the office. I need to be sure Horace is awaiting him and that Seth's trip will be completed. Seth is horrified that I suggest going inside to meet his friends that are waiting to see him off on his great adventure. I've never met these lodge buddies before now. Insisting, I open the large double doors that lead into the lodge. Three men sit in hard plastic chairs facing the door. It is a strange sight, as they all look alike with slicked-back silver hair, thin weasel-like features and false smiles. Their stares are piercing and in some way frightening. Although Seth does not look like them, I know in my heart he is exactly as these men are in the hidden parts of himself. We are told Horace is in the back room. I feel as though I have entered the heart of the "He-Man-Woman-Haters Club", and decide to leave the lobby instantly or risk being burned at a stake.

Seth escorts me outside and takes his baggage out of the back of my vehicle. He has completely calmed down at this point, lest his friends inside witness his apparent loss of control. We hug, I wish him a great trip, and watch as he wheels his suitcase toward the lodge doors. I know this is the last time I will ever have to go through verbal and emotional abuse on any level, with anyone, ever again.

Climbing back into my vehicle, I drive away as fast as possible. An enormous weight begins to lift from my body. I am free. I did this. I have worked hard on myself and my deep-rooted codependency issues to get to this point. I thank God for helping to make this moment possible.

After doing some errands, I arrive home to the phone ringing. It is Seth. Because of some mix-up, the apartment that he rented for the two months in India is now not available. He is coming home! Oh, God, what now?! He said he will wait several hours, and if things still aren't settled with the apartment, he will cancel the trip! I am near the breaking point. The clock ticks by. The hours come and go. The phone still hasn't rung with any information of his location at this point.

I leave the house and meet a friend for coffee, but I can barely hear anything she is saying. I have absolutely no energy.

Finally, returning to my home tonight, there are no telephone messages. Seth must be on the plane. I need to sleep. Good night, for now.

THE 2ND DAY

I am angry. I have done the perfect "anti-me" mantra and tell myself that I am angry for letting this abuse go on for years. No. I am changing that as of now. I am not angry with myself—I am angry with him. I need to nurture myself. I need to find a way to stop obsessing and take care of my sobriety by going to a meeting tonight. I used to think that taking care of needs meant having enough drugs and alcohol to kill the pain and the fear. There were never enough substances to do that job. I have to learn another way.

Isolating at home isn't taking care of anything. Even an on-line support group would be better than lying around reading about abusive relationships and codependency. Sometime this behavior can work in reverse, letting the anger feed on itself and become bigger. If I do not roll off this couch and do something good for myself, I'll be at a liquor store in no time. My anxiety is out of control.

Evening: Tonight I went to a meeting and received much needed support from people I know. Upon returning home I phoned my no-nonsense recovering friend, Cathy. She barked at me that what Seth did, which was to plan the whole India trip behind my back, when we were supposed to go together, was abusive and vindictive. She also said that my problem has gone way beyond codependency and into relationship addiction. Seth is my drug of choice, replacing the other substances I was using in the past. I tried to control the relationship in the same way I tried to control substances; trying to make it work at any cost. My moods and feelings of well-being would sway with the rhythm of the relationship. Cathy pointed out that I am now again at a life-or-death point. If I go back to the relationship, I may be forever lost.

THE 3ᴿᴰ DAY

Wow! What a good day it was! I went to a thrift shop and took my time. I bought a blue scarf and a few books. I then went to the library for a visiting author's talk on the book, *Quail Hill; Life on an Organic Farm.* The book had been a straight forward and precious read. After the talk and refreshments I decided to stop in at the church I am care-taker of to set up for service this Sunday. There I ran into my friend Maryann who was dropping off printed fliers for an event we were having in the future. We went inside the church and sat in the back pew. The 200 year old sanctuary's musky smell gave a calming feeling as the afternoon sun illuminated the stained glass windows with an "other worldly" glow. Dust particles danced in the beams of sunlight. We stayed and talked together for quite some time, and supported each other as we discussed our future endeavors. This evening the High School was putting on the play *Pippin*, so I attended with my friend June.

It is so nice not to feel rushed and that I have to get home as Seth may be waiting in anger while planning a retaliation because I had a night out. I thought about the conversation with Cathy last night. In all my love relationships, I have put my significant others on a pedestal. I have made them all my Higher Power. Cathy told me to knock them off and put God back up there. The thought helps me to put Seth into better perspective.

THE 4TH DAY

After reading more information about addictive and abusive relationships, I am learning that my significant other is not special or unique. He is just another garden-variety abuser. I picked up the book, *Why Does He DO That? Inside the Minds of Angry and Controlling Men,* by Lundy Bancroft. In the book, I learn that his abuse is his problem that only *he* can work on, just as my substance abuse is *my* problem than only I can work on. I did not cause or create the abuse, and I cannot control it. This is *his* problem. This concept helps me with the free-floating guilt that I have been feeling—the feeling that urges me to blame myself in some way.

I went to church this morning, another thing that Seth never liked. He said it cut into our time together and that I was hiding in religion instead of facing real problems. Pastor Dorothy's sermon was about the fear of change and standing on the edge of making a life-changing decision. She spoke about the "leap of faith" and learning who you are as a single entity. I realize I do not have any idea who I am without being a daughter, an ex-wife, a mother, a girlfriend, a boss, and so on. The sermon urges me to contemplate these questions. I asked for prayers and support.

Upon coming home this afternoon, I decide it is time to prepare the "final farewell e-mail to Seth. I write it as benign as possible, as I fear his retaliation. The e-mail states that I need to move on, and said, "thank you for all the good things that you brought into the relationship, and I will continue to build on them in the future." I hit the send button and put a "block-sender" on his address. I thought I would feel great or at least better than I have been feeling, but I do not. I feel bad. I feel sad. I hope for something better.

THE 5TH DAY

Feeling physically not well again today, I need to sleep, venturing out only to go to a meeting to ask for support. I find that people help me once again to get out of myself, out of my despair, and lessen the constant emotional pain. Wishing for a magic remedy to release these feelings, I wonder how some people just seem to breeze through events like this.

THE 6ᵀᴴ DAY

Seth called from India. I tried not to pick up the call, but I faltered. When I tried to ignore the call, the free-floating guilt feeling resurfaced. We spoke for two hours about his needing to get help for his abusive behavior, and how couple's therapy would not work until he took responsibility for the need to change. He said he does not have an abuse problem—that I have the abuse problem. Do I? I begin to doubt myself again.

He tells me he loves me, he misses me, and that he has been sick ever since he left because he did not take me with him. He sounds lonely, lost, and afraid. My warped maternal instincts start to surface and want to rescue. Eventually, we end the phone call.

Feeling totally confused, I have no idea what to do. I call my mother in Florida. She asks, "What does your heart tell you to do?" I tell her I don't have a clue what my heart is saying but that I know I can't go through any more of this. She said, "Well, you've come a long way. Stick to your decision."

The problem is I know he loves me, and I know he needs me. Then, again, what do I really know? With all the lies and behaviors that speak the exact opposite of love, what do I really know?

THE 7TH THROUGH THE 11TH DAY

Feeling horrible, I stay on the couch and watch episode after episode of *X-Files.* Mulder and Scully give me comfort. I eat chocolate cake with whipped cream and had "root canal" at the dentist. A friend once said that root canal, metaphysically speaking, represents getting to "the root of the problem". Coincidentally, I also had a tooth actually pulled for the first time in my life.

I order more books on "getting unstuck", "gaining control of your life", and relationship addiction. I swallow antibiotics for my tooth. Seth called again, but I didn't pick up the phone. I went to a meeting and then to a movie alone, but it was sold out.

It is freezing outside. I go to church and pray for relief, direction, and for these anguishing feelings to end.

THE 12ᵀᴴ DAY

"We can't solve problems by using the same
kind of thinking
we used when we created them."

—Albert Einstein

After doing even more reading on codependency and relationship addiction, I came away with the simple fact that I must change my thinking. As the saying goes, "Your best thinking got you here." My ninety-five year old friend, Carol, said, "The key is to know who you are, dear. That way, you will not bite the bait every time someone does the defining for you. You will not buy into the garbage that they tell you that you are."

There is that question again. Who am I? I have been focusing on others and on external events my whole life. I have had a lot of therapy in my life to try to answer this question, but the "pro and con" lists of my attributes and defects of character weren't helping me to know myself, and listing hobbies and writing essays about where I want to be in five years from then wasn't answering any of the core questions.

My therapists have gently explained to me that I need to be talking about myself and not my significant other, but I never seem to speak about myself outside the context of talking about the distressed relationship. I just don't know how to do this. My anxiety level is always so high that I can barely breathe, let alone think clearly. The more fearful I feel, the narrower my focus becomes. Thinking "outside the box" is impossible.

I ask myself these questions today: Do I believe I am good enough to expect goodness back? Would God want me to suffer as I have? Or do I believe that I have what it takes to be a winner? Do I believe that I can at least feel free to care for myself? Does my child deserve a healthy mother? Have I gone through all the events in my life just to be disrespected by some abusive jerk? Are others missing what I have to offer because I am always depressed, miserable, and Seth-centered as I try to exist in this unhealthy and destructive relationship?

13

When I was drinking, it was easy for my ex-husband and Seth to blame their raging on my addictions, but now I am not drinking and am recovering, and they are still raging. Abusive people have that "wonderful" side that keeps you hooked. I was always trying to control the relationship to keep that "wonderful person" from disappearing into a mean, emotionally devastating, physically violent, sexually and financially withholding monster. I am neither the cause of their problems, nor the cure. I have allowed myself to be a victim all of my life because of my thinking.

If I go back to Seth after all the new knowledge I am gaining, I will no longer be a victim of his abuse; I will be a participant in it.

THE 13TH DAY

Seth hasn't called from India for a while. My thinking immediately went to the possibility that he was with another woman. I let myself fantasize about that one for awhile. Of course, I saw her as more attractive and more capable than I am. I laughed to myself, as I suppose it is a thought that I need to get used to since I've made up my mind that I've passed the point of ever returning to the relationship.

Several times over the years, Seth has left me—sometimes for five days, or five months. He left me at least four times a year. Each time, I was emotionally devastated.

This time, however, I realize that this pattern might never end. Each time he did something hurtful, I would pick myself up and out of the resulting emotional ditch and start to feel somewhat better. Then he would do something hurtful again—and again. How much more is my sobriety and physical health supposed to take of this type of treatment? I kept hoping and praying for the big "change"—his change, of course. I thought I was just fine.

My father said something that is helpful in letting go of some of the feelings of guilt that I haven't tried hard enough or long enough to "make it work". He said, "If God wanted the two of you together, He would have put His anointing on the relationship by now." Not that my father could possibly know God's intentions, but he has a point. Several years have come and gone. I can't take another round of this. I have to accept that the situation may never change. Only I can change. I tried to change within the context of the relationship, but it wasn't possible. Seth would just hold up another hoop for me to jump through. The hoops went on into infinity.

I began playing the "did he love me, did he love me not" game. Of course he is just as incapable of having a healthy relationship as I am. Whether he loved me or not doesn't matter now. What matters is how I feel about loving myself. Maybe I will be lovable to someone else, or maybe I won't be, but I need to be alright with that. I need to see my own value. I just know that I want to feel joy and to laugh again.

I want this grief to be gentler and to let go sooner, but I know I have to go through the emotional wreckage as the prelude to the freedom and the joy that awaits on the other side of this mess. My joy wants to find expression, unencumbered. It will.

THE 16TH DAY

Reflecting more on my latest insights, I am encouraged to find that I have come a lot further in my recovery over the years than I thought. Near the end of the incredibly tangled relationship with Seth, I had begun to take better care of myself emotionally. I have taken a big step in attending "Codependents Anonymous" where I learn how to stay with any uncomfortable feelings and get a handle on them by using the tools of the program. If the feelings are too overwhelming, I pick up the phone and call a friend whom I know will understand what I am experiencing. Even though I was steadily improving myself toward the end of the relationship, Seth's behavior grew worse. I need to look at my part in the relationship and why I stayed so long if Seth refused to get help or do any real work to change his own behavior.

No matter how hard I had tried, my relationship was never going to be healthy because I was trying alone. The fact that Seth was going to India without me was not the end of the world. What finally ended the relationship for me was the deliberately hurtful and uncompromising way he delivered the news. Not only was there never a discussion about his planning the trip, his delivery was aimed to wound. After years of this type of treatment, I began to disappear spiritually. Feeling as though I didn't matter, that I was wrong in every way, and that I did not deserve anything better, I began to be physically ill from stress. The only reason he could have this type of effect on me is because my thinking was wrong. I had become warped and conditioned years before I ever met him because of the way I was taught to think about relationships. I still struggle with understanding proper self-care. Apparently it ranges from making a dental appointment, to eating healthy, stopping other addictive behaviors, learning emotional boundaries and being able to help others in a way that doesn't hurt me while trying to meet a need of someone else. Knowing how to accept healthy care from others is imperative, also. We live in community, not in a vacuum.

All I know for sure at this point is that I never again want to feel this way for "love".

THE 17TH DAY

As of this moment, I am nothing but a big crying lump on my couch. I hate myself and everything and everyone. Rage is spilling out of me over having driven to my ex-husband's house to pick up my son. An argument began with my ex, and he completely disrespected me in front of my son. Being in an emotionally vulnerable place, I was not prepared to deal with the usual degrading treatment I receive from him.

I turn over on the couch and try to get a hold on my emotions. I see the blinking light of the answering machine. Seth had called. I certainly didn't feel like listening to his message, but I did. He was leaving me instructions on where to leave his key to his house-watching job that I was taking over for him in his absence. The message is emotionally empty, confirming my feelings of being unlovable. I call my 95 year old friend, Carol, and cry all my pain into the phone. She said, "Why should you expect your ex-husband to be considerate of your feelings now? He never was before!" She is right. This is why we are not married any longer. She goes on to say, "You don't have to listen to any more of Seth's messages. You do not owe him one thing. Being finished with someone is being finished. Of *course* you are loveable, or you and I wouldn't be such good friends. Just because your ex-husband and Seth do not appreciate or see your value does not mean that other people don't see it. You are the one that needs to see your value, not anyone else." Again, she is right.

Piecing myself back together again, I realize that part of being free is being free to choose. I had a choice in how to act at my ex-husband's house, and listening or not listening to Seth's message. In both cases I chose the more self-destructive path, acting out of fear and guilt instead of self-love and dignity. I will be more mindful the next time.

THE 18ᵀᴴ TO THE 24ᵀᴴ DAY

These last four days went by quickly. In the first three days, I felt great after releasing all those negative emotions a short time ago. But today, I feel as bad as I did when I first started this journey. I guess the grief process must be like this—ebbing and flowing like a tide.

"Fear of abandonment" is the latest topic I am reading about. Abandonment is a huge block to me in letting go and trusting God. Sitting in my favorite arm chair, I put the book down on my lap, and reflect on the past. At the end of the relationship with Seth, I felt I had worked through many of my abandonment issues, but now I realize that Seth was just the first layer of this onion I am peeling. Because of the constant distraction a dysfunctional relationship can provide, I am oblivious to all the underlying, unresolved issues in my past and primary relationships. My substance abuse helped me to mask the pain of my codependency, and my relationship addiction provided relief from focusing on myself and on my own unhealed emotional problems. To have other's approval, I had to change to fit *their* criteria rather than me looking for my own worth and approval, or risk abandonment. I lost sight of my true being.

It is not Seth that I miss. It is the fantasy and the dream that I hung on to, which wasn't even close to the real situation. Thinking that eventually I would find the diamond at his core I hung in there, only to find out that there is no diamond. Deep inside, he is one big scrambled mess of a disordered person. The diamonds are within us, but working on ourselves is what exposes them rather than just stumbling upon one. A substance abuse counselor once said to me, "This is Self-Help. You have to help yourself; no one else is going to do that for you." I want to be guided by faith and trust to find my own answers that wait within me. I will teach myself to listen to my own intuition and to trust that still, small voice. For now, I just pray to stay open to all possibilities of what will appear on my path.

There is a piece of the Divine in us all, and I am letting the Divine guide me to re-connect with the core of my true nature; the person God intended me to be.

THE 25ᵀᴴ DAY

This afternoon I trudge in the snow between my house and the garage and pack up all of Seth's belongings'. The only sound outside is the crunching of the snow, my breathing, and the final bang and click of the closing vehicle trunk. Not wanting to risk going to his apartment and seeing his landlady, and the possibility of re-running any scenes from the past in my mind, I drive to the house-watching job. I leave his items in the oil-burner room, along with the key, and lock the door behind me. Again, I hear the crunching of the snow under foot as I walk away from this nightmare. I send him an e-mail telling him where he can pick up his stuff, and there will be no reason to come to my home ever again. Wow! The final step has been taken.

Having worked through the self-imposed guilt of ending the relationship and my false sense of obligation to him, I realize it is all rules that I made up; all the guilt and obligation came from my own imagination. Seth never was committed to me. I just believed his lies. Ralph Waldo Emerson wrote, "How can I hear what you are saying when your actions are thundering in my ears?" When I think back, all the signs pointed to his not being a faithful partner, but I didn't want to see that. It hurt too much. I needed another brain scrubbing. Even if he is with someone else, what does it matter now?

The number 333 used to be a symbol for us that meant, "I love you." I recently keep seeing 333 in various places. Feeling there is a message in this synchronicity, I become quiet and just listen for what comes up from my inner knowing. I hear the words, "Let go with love." If I let go with love, I am truly free. Any bad feelings that I harbor will hurt only me. What I believe, think, and feel will be drawn back to me in some way. What we believe and think is what we experience.

In my recovery reading, I learn about the bonding chemical, oxytocin. The chemical, located in the brain, begins to recede after an addiction is given up, a relationship has ended, or anything else that a person feels strongly bonded to is taken away. The lack of this chemical produces withdrawal symptoms which can explain why I was not only in emotional pain, but physical pain as well. I know from past experience this is usually a three month process for me.

Friends tell me that they believe "duty dating" is the answer to lessen the withdrawal, but I can't think of anything more repulsive than dating someone in whom I have no interest. If I do find someone in whom I am interested, I'll just be setting up the same cycle in embracing another way to take the focus off the real situation and feelings; another temporary bandage to mask the pain.

"What about sex," they ask. "Don't you miss it?" Long ago, a mentor of mine said that energy isn't something compartmentalized. It is a whole, and we can channel it where needed. She said to use my sexual energy in a creative manner. So I've channeled it into thinking about creativity and getting back into my art work. My sexual energy is now helping to feed my creative drive.

Deciding to stay single and learn how to have a relationship with just me is what I need to do for now in order to learn and heal. Tomorrow I am leaving for Florida on a vacation with my son. The change of scenery will do me good.

THE 44TH DAY

Florida was good for the soul. The sweet smell of the air and the comforting Spanish moss hanging from various trees, made time feel irrelevant. The vacation was only for five days, and my son and I took the train. The train can be tough, but it was great to spend time with him and reconnect. One of my most anguishing regrets is how my son was cheated out of an emotionally present mother. I was spending so much time in emotional and physical misery that I could not be present for him no matter how much I tried.

During my marriage, my inability to cope with the relationship was so severe, that I suffered adrenal exhaustion along with other debilitation physical maladies. After numerous doctor visits and no solutions, I decided to take the alternative medicine route and was lead to study acupuncture and herbal medicine. Over time, I was able to correct a lot of my symptoms, but my body was still very responsive to negative stress. Therefore, the mini-vacation was a good way to take care of myself at this point.

Spring is coming and it is time to start focusing on going back to regular work. Only a year ago, I was working in a job that I needed to re-evaluate due to lack of advancement opportunities. The stress from my relationship with Seth was taking another toll on my health at this point, and I had no energy to look for another job. I still didn't know what I wanted to do "when I grew up", but I was the happiest and most relaxed while doing gardening. The garden feeds me on every level. The only problem was I had no professional experience in the horticulture field.

I began faxing resumes and making phone calls in regard to ads in the paper. Nothing was happening in terms of making headway with a response from any gardening companies. I needed to take a leap of faith. I had no 'plan B', but faith is just a leap from 'A' without having a 'B'. God will provide the 'B'. I put in my resignation with a two week notice and prayed to God to help me to land on my feet, wherever that may be.

The next day at work something unexpected happened. A woman who works in horticulture came in to the store, who knew I was looking for a job, and handed me a slip of paper with a phone number on it. I called the number and set up an interview. The following day, I was on my way to meet Alex, whom I hoped would be my next employer.

The ride out to the greenhouse for the interview was beautiful. I passed a field with grazing buffalo—for some reason, that really made an impression, which I logged away in the back of my mind. Around the bend from the buffalo was the greenhouse, and Alex came out to greet me. He was young, professional and very nice as we toured all the propagating and growing houses. Beautiful annuals grew everywhere. I was so naïve about the industry that I didn't recognize a single plant, but I knew I could learn. He congratulated me on getting the job, and we shook hands. I went home very excited and optimistic. The buffalo came to mind again. Curiously, I went on-line and looked up the metaphysical meaning of the buffalo. It read, "Prayers answered".

THE 50TH DAY

This is the first day of my five-week horticulture class. Being in a classroom always is a comfort to me as the learning environment works to get me out of my own head and into the world around me. Meeting new people is also stimulating and welcome. Yesterday, I was excited to go to an Organic Trade Show where I saw some people I knew from the class today and others I had met last year from being around the business. All sorts of synchronistic and esoteric things seemed to be occurring during the show that were signposts telling me I am on the right path.

Last year, after the season was over at the greenhouse, Alex helped me find a job at a retail nursery. The place was beautiful, but the other women weren't very receptive to me. Their attitudes may have been a result of me probably being a royal pain, as I do not know as much as they do about plants. I am hoping it will be better there this year when I return and maybe this class will help me fit in more.

Looking back over the last ten years, I think about all the missed opportunities because of my addictions and my relationship with Seth. I passed over many friendships, interesting events, and time with my son, as I had no time to nurture any of it. Because of the recent changes I've made in faith and courage, I see more doors opening, and life feels richer. Through these adventures and tests of character, I am finding out *who I am.*

At home tonight, I pull a Rune Stone from its red pouch and read the message. The stone's counsel says the old way of doing things is over. If I repeat the old way, I will suffer. The last sentence tells me to see the humor in things, stay centered, and to keep moving forward.

THE 58TH DAY

It is now two months since Seth left, and he is back from India. I see him driving today and I'm pretty sure he sees me, but he just keeps staring straight ahead. He looks the same as when I last saw him—he is wearing the same pullover and mirrored sunglasses. He continues driving past me. For some reason I don't feel much of anything. I think back to when I had to rely on him for transportation in my very early sobriety. The abuse I subjected myself to was frightening. He would scream, pound his fist on the dashboard, or choke me with one hand while driving with the other hand. He would pull the truck over in dark, barren places or unfamiliar towns and tell me to get out and actually leave me somewhere and drive home without me. He has thrown hot coffee in my face as I sat in the passenger side and has left me standing in the extreme pouring rain, getting soaked by passing vehicles splashing through curb puddles, while waiting for him to pick me up when he had no intensions of coming. More than one time, my poor old friend Carol had to drive to get me and let me spend the night at her home.

All I know—and what really matters—is that I want to be finished with Seth. I need to let go of the heavy resentment I've been dragging around, but that requires forgiveness and wishing him well and I haven't reached that point yet. No matter how much I pray for the willingness to "let go with love," I just stay stuck. I've read that if we see ourselves as victims, the ego will hang on to whatever resentment it needs to keep the energy going to the victim role. I suppose I still feel like a victim, but I want to feel like a survivor.

My resentment isn't only because he treated me badly, but because I lost my dream. I just knew if I waited long enough, tried hard enough, that love would overcome all and he would stop hurting me once he had gratitude that I was always there for him. He would get down on one knee, and finally propose with the diamond ring I wanted and would care for us the way a grown man who truly loves a woman would care. Instead he used me, and I let him do it. Perhaps the forgiveness I need to find in order to let go of this resentment is to start with forgiving *me*, since all things begin with the self. I need to forgive myself for allowing him to mistreat my son, my family, my friends, and me and for having stayed in the relationship way past its expiration date. Forgiveness and moving on are processes that take time.

On a talk show program, a famous former supermodel confided that she had been in an emotionally abusive relationship. At work and around her friends and family, she felt great, but with her abusive boyfriend, she felt terrible. Even as a top model, she had suffered from low self-esteem, which had her stuck in the relationship. When she looked in the mirror one day, she said, "I have to leave this . . ." it still took time to make the move. Yes, it is a process, but process we must.

THE 60ᵀᴴ DAY

While sitting in my vehicle in Carol's driveway waiting for her to join me for lunch, I pick up my affirmation book and pray, "Okay, God, show me what it is that you want me to know." Every page I flip open has something to do with Love. I glance down at my console and there is a discarded wrapper with the word "Love" written on it. "All right . . ." I pray again, "Please show me the message I need to understand." The next time I open the book, it says, "The struggle to love one another may be a daily one for us, and it is made more difficult because we still stumble in our attempts to love ourselves."

People often say to me that I "lack self-esteem." I really have no idea what "self-esteem" means. I will think of the word, but no feeling follows because *I have no self-esteem.* In the past I was determined to "get" the self-esteem that everyone else seemed to understand, but Carol told me, "Dear, you don't go out and *get* self-esteem. You already possess it within you. You just need to learn to uncover it."

This remark brought me back to years before when I had read about the theory of the "inner-child". The exercises in the book were supposed to help the person learn to love themselves by starting with remembering the hurt inner child that we abandoned. It wasn't until years later, during my last recovery adventure, that I really got to work and wanted to solve this self-love, self-esteem problem. I resurrected the book from a dusty shelf and began again.

These lessons started to take hold internally, and I began communicating with my hurt inner child, which I had abandoned when she was ten years old out of shame. I left her behind. With the exercises, however, I began reconnecting with her, little by little. In doing so, I began to learn to comfort and nurture the adult "me". I started to get a glimmer of what self-esteem feels like. It feels *good,* it feels *solid,* and I want more of it. I was still with Seth at the time during this birthing process, and it made the journey so much more difficult. Since I was still far away from being stable enough to end the relationship, I tried using his abuse as a way to grow stronger. The internal dialogue was, "Okay, Seth, I am going to prove you wrong. I know you want me to fail so you can keep looking better than I am. However, I am going to keep growing in my recovery and in my life in spite of you." This proved to be exhausting. I spent hours—sometimes days—soothing myself from his horrible tirades and threats of abandonment.

I am fortunate to have stayed sober through that time. Today, it is so much easier and rewarding to feel good about myself and about my accomplishment of beginning to be included in an amazing support system with a great group of friends who are encouraging and honest, rather than with an abusive lover. This new circle of friends did not just appear out of no-where. I met them and fostered the connection. This comes from learning how to make healthy choices that are in line with *who you are.*

THE 62ND DAY

Last night I decided to go to an Earthsave potluck dinner. For some reason I am afraid about going alone. I've gone to many other places alone, but I feel intimidated on this particular evening.

After parking, and finally finding the right door to go in, a woman is taking the money or the food for the event and welcomes me warmly. Her name is Stephanie. She has a harsh, but attractive appearance and energy with her tied back black hair and dark brown eyes. Her tall, thin stature requires her to lean over the paperwork on the table to sign me in to the event. As I sit down at one of the long tables in a room with tiled floors, walls and ceilings, a few more people trickle in. Behind the incoming group, I see my friend from the Organic Trade Show, Steve. He is the organic instructor and founder of The Organic Lyceum. I get up and give him a hug, which is reciprocated. The gathering soon turns out to be the most comfortable group of people as we all relax and eat delicious vegan food and had stimulating conversation. Sitting next to a bee keeper named Tom, I listen as he talked about how the bees survived this cold weather and he would be organizing nature walks in the spring.

On my way home, I think about how the evening would have gone if I had been there with Seth. He wouldn't have enjoyed the company and complained that they weren't of equal caliber to him. He probably would have insulted them, making it impossible for me to ever go back to another monthly dinner. My conversations with Steve and Tom could not have taken place, as Seth would have been jealous. And if he hadn't come with me, I'd have been watching the clock, afraid to stay too long, and would have raced home to ward off any retaliation for having to good of a time.

This morning, my son comes over for pancakes. We sit at the table and spoke about his Catholic confirmation ceremony coming up this spring, and the party we will plan for him. The time I spend with my son is sacred to me. As he gets older, and more handsome, he'll be a grown man before I know what happened. Since today is Sunday, if I were with Seth, I would never be having this breakfast time with my son, as Sunday's were always Seth's day. He felt competitive with my son, and I was always walking on egg shells with the two of them, never knowing how things were going to turn out by the end of the day.

Church is on the agenda, another event that Seth hated my attending. Part of the sermon is from Exodus 20:17. "You shall not covet your neighbor's hours, your neighbors wife, or male or female slave, or donkey, or anything that belongs to your neighbor." My mind jumps to all the other things we shouldn't covet either, such as someone's bad behavior, abuse, jealousy, complaining, and badgering. I am learning to let the other person keep what is his and not to take responsibility for it.

Another reading, from Matthew 14:3-8 was about Mary's using oil of spikenard to anoint Jesus before his death. Judas objected, as he felt it was a waste of the costly oil and it could be sold and the money given to the poor. Jesus said, "Let her alone. She has kept this for the day of my burial. For the poor you will have with you always, but Me, you do not have always."

This reading leads me to realize that life is precious. We have our lives here on earth for only a short, short time . . . and I want mine to count for something.

THE 65TH DAY

This afternoon I drive to the other side of town to visit my friend Ida, who had requested a copy of a book I've read called, *The Secret Life of Plants*. Ida and I had both taken The Organic Lyceum's horticulture course where one of the classes taught that man is co-creator with the earth, complete with garden divas, nature spirits, and elementals. *The Findhorn Garden* is also one of my favorite reading recommendations. My garden is where I am the most in touch with nature, my thoughts and God.

Upon arriving at Ida's house for the first time, I was awestruck by the fact that I was looking at a $2.5 million dollar home with at least one full acre of land impeccably kept by a gardener. Once inside her home, I was taken in by the beauty of her earth-toned dining room that seated eight people, her tennis court, swimming pool, and guest house in the back yard, her bio-dynamic vegetable garden, and other luxuries.

What I admire the most about Ida is that she is self-made. The company she owns makes banners out of recycled waste. Commercial buildings, stadiums and museums are her customers. "Think abundance," is one of Ida's usual sayings. She works from home and is disciplined enough to do so.

My home is small, but I only need to use three of its five rooms. I forget about the living room and the den, as most of my work is done in the bedroom at my desk. My home has become emotionally safe for me. Entering the house after a long day, I can close the door and have peace now. The feeling I have here is one of expansion—my consciousness expanding with my personal growth. My breath is calm; my body is relaxed. I am learning to know myself through the experience of living alone. When I think of the tirades of abuse that had taken place here, I would never trade what I have now for that ever again. If I ever feel lonely, I can go to an event, a meeting, go on email, or call someone. I need to be my own best company, because in the end I am all I have. Wherever I go, there I am.

THE 71ST DAY

I am now in uncharted territory. Never before have I been in this particular inner place. I've learned in this past year how to get off the merry-go-round. But now that I'm off, I don't know where I am.

Nothing is familiar. I would like to call this the "dark night of the soul", but it is much more than that. There are parts of me that have been cut off and buried. I can actually feel these covered places within me, but I don't know what they are or what they want to express.

Just as a butterfly must cocoon itself before becoming its most beautiful self, any transformation has a gestation period. I am now waiting to see who I am without all those negative influences. For years, I have been wrapped up in blankets of lies, my own and other people's lies. It is time to go within to see who and what is there, and what has been waiting a very long time for it to be safe to come out. Living in my head isn't going to get me into my heart. T.S. Eliot described those covered and blank spaces inside of us as "vacant interstellar spaces", but they aren't vacant. They are just hiding in the dark.

I've been eyeing the meditation space that I set up in the living room that I have yet to use. Meditation has always intimidated me. Pastor Dorothy asked me if I was afraid that once I went within I may have to give up something, or change something. A popular spiritual guru once said we aren't afraid of being inadequate as much as we are afraid of how powerful we are. Being powerful means being responsible for our decisions and being able to bring about change.

Maybe I am afraid that whatever lies unexpressed within will blossom to the surface and take on a life of its own. Then I will have to nurture it and be responsible for it, what ever "it" is. However, what else is there to do? Spiritual growth always moves us forward, and I know that it will take more energy to stand still than to let the tide carry me to where I am meant to go.

THE 72ND DAY

Another terrible bout of anger descended upon me about Seth. No matter what I did, I just couldn't get out of that space. I felt like a transmission locked in a certain gear that no amount of force could free it. Resentment and feelings of revenge are poison to the soul. Ida once said, "Be careful of your thoughts! They are like micro-waves. Seth will pick up on them, and then you'll even have a *more* challenging situation". If you believe in Quantum Physics, she is correct. But how do I get rid of these feelings, I asked Ida. She said, "Just say 'cancel, cancel' every time the memories and feelings come." But that wasn't working, either.

Later in the evening, I remembered her words about thoughts emitting on universal waves, and I wonder, "What if *he* is the one sending resentful thoughts my way, and I am picking up on them!?" Immediately, I imagine being surrounded by light and love, and see myself holding up a mirror and letting his thoughts reflect back to him. The results are amazing! Instantly my anger and resentment, which match the size of Manhattan, dissolved! I do not know if it is the power of imagery or the power of suggestion, or that the energy of thought really is that powerful, but it worked. If going within and meditating is what I need to be doing, I will be careful not to let negative energy from an outside source invade my space.

PART II

THE IN-BETWEEN

THE KING OF THE BUTTERFLIES

Seated by the labyrinth's edge
Pairs of Monarchs fly by.
The Monarch knows when it is time to go.
And they know where they are going . . .
although they've never been there before.

Riding the push of the cold front
The Monarch travels
stopping only to savor the nectar
of the inviting plants.

Riding the push of the never ending
creative energy into the
endless unfolding of existence
my choice is the same as the Monarch . . .
pausing only for survival to make the journey,
which is the ultimate survival.

To stop, is to die.

The bliss at the arrival
of the destination
is known only to the Monarch.
And within the bliss
again is the hard work of continuation.

Overhead, their journey is in clusters . . .
my heart goes with them . . .
for they travel with a deep knowing
what their purpose is.

Those butterflies know more than I.
And I envy them.

THE 75ᵀᴴ DAY

I am finally back to work at the plant nursery, hoping to become lost in the growing and selling of plants. This is a chance to be carried off and away from the painful events of the Seth saga.

An umbrella is attached overhead to the soil bin in front of me, as it is pouring rain today. The soil is becoming saturated and soon I am scooping nothing but mud into the planting containers. Somehow, in spite of the rain gear, I am getting soaked. From behind the hill that separates our nursery from the train tracks, the smell of a dead deer wafts up since being killed by a train in the middle of the night. As physically miserable as I feel, I keep trying to convince myself that I am enjoying this job, even though my three co-workers, Daisy, Rose, and Iris, are working in the greenhouse and keeping dry and warm. I pray for the feeling of gratitude that I even have a job.

Since completing my horticulture program over the winter, I was hoping for a raise in pay. My bi-weekly paycheck was no longer covering my living expenses. But for some reason, the emotional atmosphere was thick with tension. Asking for a pay raise did not feel like the right move at this time.

The existing tension could have something to do with my boss Gert and her husband being at serious odds. She found out her husband was probably having an affair. Gert, a woman with a sight build, plain features, and classy demeanor, is another emotionally, verbally, and perhaps physically abused woman. It seems amazing to me that I am in a work situation that is much the same as my home situation was. Watching Gert's interaction with her husband makes my mouth drop open with disbelief; it is as if I am witnessing my own relationship in the third person. However, Gert does not intend to leave him. She is doing the pretzel dance—going to therapy and bending over backward to change herself in order to tolerate her situation.

To make matters even more challenging, there is no shift in the attitudes of my three co-workers since last season. They are very bonded, and make subtle remarks that indicate I am not part of their sphere. Because of my lack of experience in this field, I feel stuck at the moment. I pray for God to help me to stick with the situation, to learn the business, and to fit in.

THE 80ᵀᴴ DAY

Today is my son Anthony's Catholic confirmation, and a perfect day it is! The church is packed with standing room only. My son's turn to read arrived. Standing beside the alter and behind the speaker's podium, he looks so handsome at fifteen years old. The suit he and I picked out for the special occasion was stunning, and his delivery of the long speech goes down without a flaw. Sitting in the pew mid-way in the church, I let my mind drift back to his First Communion when he was seven years old. I was still with Seth at that time, and still drinking. Thankfully, I am now sober, but my heart sinks when I think about what Anthony must have went through during the ups and downs with his father, the divorce, the drinking, and the doomed relationship with Seth. Shame rears its ugly head when I remember these scenarios.

Perhaps the only reason he made it through all these terrible events is that he had a lot of healthy support. My ex-husband and I sent him to a great counselor during the divorce so he had a trusted outside adult to talk to, as his parents were useless at that time. He had good friends and grandparents who love him. He knows his father and I love him, too, despite what was happening in our marriage. Love does heal. Anthony is turning into a fine young man, and his father and I are both very proud of him.

My relationship with God is growing daily. I've come to realize that having a relationship with God is just like any other relationship. It needs time, attention, communication, and nurturing every day. I am learning to trust, and if I can't trust God to have good intentions for me, whom can I trust? I need to remember that Anthony has his own Higher Power who works in his life and is there for him. Since I cannot change the past, all I can do is commit to being present to Anthony and supportive of his growth. God and my son forgive me, but I haven't yet forgiven myself, or I wouldn't feel such shame. I need to work on forgiving myself and everyone else, although it may take a lifetime.

THE 85TH DAY

In my life's quest for answers, I have learned about many different forms of religion and spirituality. I was raised Catholic, but I never felt anything in those pews to write home about. Branching out into other belief systems, I explored Eastern religion, American Indian philosophy, New Age, Wicca, and more. Eventually I came back full circle to rediscover the Bible and the teachings of Jesus. Jesus knew how to work the Universal Laws. Science of Mind is also a wonderful teaching promoted by Ernest Holms, who also speaks of Jesus. This philosophy focuses on the Universal Laws and the power of our thoughts.

Recently, I've come to understand why the Bible is referred to as "the Living Word". While studying passages with Pastor Dorothy, the same passage would take on new meaning over time. I found the passage would work on me, rather than me working on it. The passage gave life.

The Twelve Steps in recovery programs seem to work in the same way. The more one grows in recovery, the more and different meanings there are in each step.

This idea reminds me of when I took a small hand mirror and held it up to a bigger mirror. The reflection went on into infinity. In the same way as that reflection presents itself, the spiritual journey is vast, huge, and never ending. The best part is that the journey doesn't have to be taken alone. Many helpers appear along the path. Support awaits the traveler in many forms.

THE 94TH DAY

It is said that it takes ninety days to break a habit. I am now four days past the mark. My healing process is further along now that I am not lingering in an anguishing relationship. Seth is still out of sight since his return from India except for the one time that I caught a glimpse of him driving his truck. It is "business as usual" for him, I guess. Coming across a journal that I had written three years ago, I cringe at the entries about Seth, but I am grateful that I no longer experience those feelings. Seth is definitely the 'Wizard of Oz', the little man behind the curtain who I allowed to spin my reality.

An entry reads, "If he leaves me, what will I feel? Likely I will feel anxiety, panic, and guilt. If he stays, what will I feel? Probably relief, thinking that all is okay and that I must be lovable. However, soon after the feeling that all is 'okay', I will start to feel confused, off balance, and depressed. These feelings are what he seems to want me to feel. I allow him to manipulate me by having access to my weak points and fears. He is always on this balance beam with me—one foot in the relationship and one foot out. As the saying goes, 'when one foot is out, they are both really out'."

Another entry reads, "Instead of always focusing on how he feels and what he may be thinking, I need to think about what I am feeling and thinking. I feel devoured. If things are 'good', it leads me to eventually feel used up by his demands and neediness. When things go 'bad', I feel violated and devoured by my own shock, rage, and anguish. Looking back on all my relationships I feel that I have always been with the 'same man'. They follow the same blueprint . . . the same play produced over and over again. What is it that God wants me to learn from these painful lessons? I want to choose differently, but how? These feelings remind me of my childhood relationships. Am I choosing events that will match the old feelings and behavior patterns of my life? Seth said he is coming over tonight. He sounded angry on the phone. I wonder if he is even going to show up. His only possessions in my house are his yellow shorts. I know how important those yellow shorts are to him, so I know he will show up eventually even if it is only to pick up his shorts. A vehicle door just shut. He's here . . . !"

I can only think about how pathetic these trains of thought were . . . .

Another entry read, "If I were anyone else, would you scream, yell, and slam the brakes on while you're driving? If I were anyone else, would you cancel dinner at the last minute without explanation? Would you say things that make me cry more than I already am? When I step off my 'platform' where I feel healthy, it is the equivalent to falling into a pool of man-eating fish where you're trying to hold me down to be eaten. It feels like you are lurking in the shadows, waiting for a hint of weakness so you can finish me off, as if I were a wounded animal. You steady me just enough to make the fall more pleasurable for you. It feels the same as when you fatten up the ducks before you hunt them.

Another entry read, "I keep rehearsing the words over and over to be able to say, 'This is not working out. This really isn't going anywhere.' Will I ever be able to say these words to you and mean them? Whenever I hint at them or struggle to say them, I am too indirect. Then you hurry to reassure me that all is well and that I am just hurting myself by even thinking these thoughts. Then I am pulled into denial and feel that film glaze over me, or I get a complete anxiety attack because I think I should be considering your feelings and not just mine. Someone else's feelings are involved, and what if I am wrong? What if it is just my pathology as you say it is? Am I just being selfish, or are my needs not being fulfilled? Am I spending too much time thinking about it?"

The next entry, "Well, you did it again! Where do you get off treating my hospitality the way you did tonight at dinner? Where do you get off treating my son that way? Then you left—ran away—expecting me to call or else be here when *you* call. You would never tolerate that behavior from *me*. You destroy things that have the potential to be good. I want to unhook! I can't understand why I haven't! I have new goals now. I need to fragment you and to keep sectioning our relationship into pieces until it ceases to exist! Then when the last small piece is there, I will somehow find closure."

The second to last entry, "Being a single, working mother of a pre-teen can sometimes be more of a challenge on some days than other days. At the end of the day, a woman may look to her mate for maybe just a hug;

something to help her feel supported. But again, you let me down by not being here for me. The sex we had the other night was excellent, and it made me forget for a time that we really aren't that close anymore. But now you tell me the sex was just for fun, and not to be mistaken for true intimacy. I tell you that our relationship must mature or dissolve, and you are silent. I need to face the reality that you are incapable of a true and intimate relationship, at least with me. I must, and will move on. I want to thrive, but even just surviving is difficult because of the feelings that come up inside of me pertaining to you. The part of my life that includes you is not working. It is an enormous effort to make the rest of my life work when it is being drastically affected by the one part that doesn't work—namely, this relationship."

The last entry read, "I decided I am going to insist that you honor your commitment to me, not just when you feel like it, but most of the time. Please just do what you say you are going to do. I tell you for the last time that the fundamentals of this relationship need to change—no more smoke-screen arguments to hide your real feelings or intentions. When you press on with the same, ineffective arguments, I take back the keys to my house. You say, "It's over!", and for a change I am the one who walks out of your apartment. It feels good to be the one leaving for a change."

Sadly, all these entries were all dated within a month's time. The relationship continued for another three years, but I sought help a year and a half after writing these entries. It took time to apply what I was learning in Codependents Anonymous and to finally break free. The best part was at the very end by pulling the rug out from under the whole mess and letting Seth have his way, and walking away; never having to hang on for that horrible ride again.

I thank God every day that I am getting my sanity back and sketching out a new life for myself for the first time in a healthy way. Soon the sketch will turn into a beautiful painting.

THE 112TH DAY

Working at the nursery has been grinding, wet, and slow. Business has been in a decline this year and Gert's mood has deteriorated. She chastised me by calling me a 'complete disaster' when I was trying to re-learn the cash register. I am often isolated from the work crew and given humiliating tasks, such as mowing the grass by the parking area where gravel flies up and dings customer's cars—along with my legs and face. The other women get the more prestigious and important jobs.

Gert's gruff and condescending manner makes me wonder if she plans on keeping me through the season. I've also noticed that one day Daisy acts like my best friend, and the next day I'm invisible to her. Another time, I saw her verbally attacking a customer. The woman was so taken aback by the sudden outburst that she backed up and tripped over the plant wagon, almost landing on the gravel path.

Confiding in Daisy that I am concerned that Gert may fire me, Daisy replies, "Oh no, she wouldn't do that. She knows how desperately you need this job." The statement hits me like falling bricks. Do I really need this job "desperately"? Suddenly, I feel trapped, and my instincts immediately go to "plan B". I must have an exit plan. I start praying for guidance.

THE 154TH DAY

While working behind the central barn among the exotic annuals, I look down at a paver that reads, "No occupation is as delightful to me as the culture of the earth, and no culture comparable to that of the garden." The quote by Thomas Jefferson brought me back to the beginning of my horticulture career when I knew that saying to be true. Now, however, I have to force myself to stay in this nursery.

It has only been one year ago that I was working in the dead-end job and put out prayers to help me find a different place of employment. That was when Jean gave me the phone number to Alex's greenhouse. I think about the beautiful landscape that I drove through on my way to work every day with Alex and the meaning of the buffalo. I remember sitting by my truck during lunch break and looking over the amazing array of beautiful plants and realizing I had created this experience with the help of God. I had succeeded in changing my reality. I felt that the right path was before me. Why, then am I so miserable now?

As I ponder that thought, a big tractor-trailer pulls into the nursery, loaded with more plants. Whenever this happens we are all to gather at the rear of the truck to unload. Gert, Daisy, Rose, and Iris, all come running from different directions to help. Daisy jumps into the back of the truck with the driver and they begin handing us pots, pots, and more pots. They are large, heavy plants, and the process needs to be done very quickly so the driver can be on his way. It's starting to rain again, and I ask Daisy to hand me a particular grouping of plants. She sharply replies, "Don't you tell me what to do!" I say, "Why don't you just do it yourself then?" I walk away, shaking and furious.

I walk behind one of the portable latrines and start crying. I have had enough. It completely eludes me how I keep ending up in the same victim role no matter how hard I try to change the situation. I still had no "plan B". I think about how I had walked away from the dead-end job last year with nothing more than faith. I become quiet and still and listen. From deep inside myself I hear, "Two weeks. Just wait two more weeks." I am learning to trust my inner voice. Taking a deep breath, I compose myself and go back to the truck. I wonder if Gert will fire me for walking away, but she does not. I say a prayer of gratitude and go back to work.

THE 168TH DAY

Today marks two weeks since I asked for help and guidance in finding another job, and nothing is happening yet. I have done the pavement pounding with resumes and made phone calls. It is not easy to find something mid-way into the season. Staying silent and listening for inner guidance, I keep getting the message, "Just wait . . . just wait . . ."

While working down by the river, using organic weed killer on the gravel path, I gaze across the water to the opposite shore. Memories surface of Seth fishing along the river last season comes to mind. The recall of that time together is euphoric. He would wave to me from across the river, and I would wave back. After I finished work, we would meet down river where he kept his very small boat and cast for sunfish; throwing them back into the water once we caught them. When the sun began to set, dragonflies abounded, a chorus of frogs would begin their recital, and turtles would raise their heads out of the water from time to time.

Then I remember when we would go to the museum on the weekend, one of our favorite places, and I started missing him. Romantic feelings came rushing in with full force. I look across the river again, but only see the stillness of the trees on this hot day, and rings on the water where dragonflies play in a world all their own.

THE 169TH DAY

Every morning before going to work, my routine is to stop at the same deli to get my coffee. After leaving the deli, I am waiting at the intersection at a red light when, out of nowhere, Seth pulls up to my driver side window going in the opposite direction. My window is down, and the red light allows no escape. His face is contorted with rage and a string of obscenities pours from his mouth. The light turns green, and I drive on.

It happened so fast that I feel no emotion. I find myself starting to laugh and I shake my head in disbelief. That episode is a far cry from the euphoric recall from yesterday! God was showing me, "You want him? Here he is!" I thank the Universe for telling me the truth of what I am really missing.

PART III

THE BEGINNING

IN THE LINES OF THE LABYRINTH

I see the Day open with Colored Light.
A blank canvas that holds all possibilities.
Like a Pinky-Swear promise, never to be broken.

The sweet smell and delicate sound of Nature
assures me that there is still life
as I float away from the past.
I am part of all that is.
I am all that is.
I am . . .

No cruel words circle my orbit.
Or dive into my ears.
No need to hide my heart or shut my mouth.
No self-defense tactics needed.
No thinking fast on my toes.
No frosty stares.
Only Dancing is required here.

I am alone with all there is.
I hold the possibilities.
I *AM.*

THE 186TH DAY

After another day of keeping my self-restraint during working hours at the nursery, I came home exhausted and threw myself onto the outdoor lounge chair to listen to my voice mail.

I could not believe what I was hearing! After all my efforts of pounding the pavement with resume in hand, the call was about a job offer! Again, what paid off was word of mouth, as the call was from Pam, an organic gardener and lecturer with the The Lyceum School. Steve had suggested to Pam to call me about working with her, as she had just lost her foreperson. I return the call and after chatting for about ten minutes and explaining that I will need to give the nursery at least a weeks notice, we set up an interview.

I went inside to read one of Pam's brochures that I had picked up from the Lyceum two years ago. It said, "The majority of people were brought up to believe that a perfectly manicured carpet-like lawn is a symbol of success and pride. But just as we're thinking differently about many things—the food we eat, the cars we drive, the habits that we keep—we're also thinking differently about lawns.

"Beautiful landscaping is no longer all about sterile green grass. It is about wildflowers that softly sway in the breeze. It's about feathery grasses over which butterflies float. It's about happy little hummingbirds that hover and dart while drinking sweet nectar from bountiful blossoms.

"In the garden that nature intended, grass grows in all shapes, sizes and colors, and it bustles with life and beauty in many different forms, unaided by fertilizers, pesticides and irrigation.

"Imagine dragonflies weaving around the sun's rays, the light reflecting off their delicate, lacy wings and multi-colored bodies. Imagine heavenly songbirds singing sweetly all around you, safely building their nests, encouraging their young to fly, and eating seeds and berries from the trees, shrubs, and flowers. Imagine rows of lettuce, tomatoes, and string beans and patches of raspberries, blueberries, or strawberries where you can eat fresh from the vine until you are full. Imagine your children full of confidence and strength as they climb a native tree and full of curiosity and wonder as they discover a box turtle, a ladybug, a chipmunk, or a toad.

Imagine no longer having to manage the life support that turf grass requires—no more irrigation, no more fertilizing and spraying, no more mowing or edging, and no more leaf raking. This is a barefoot garden."

For the five years that I am gardening at home, Seth would always ask, "Why are you letting weeds grow to see what kind of flower they have on them? Why are you mixing vegetables in a flower garden? Why are you building those gardens in the middle of the lawn? You are behaving like someone who just got let out of an asylum and needs something to do to keep busy." But I love it all. I feel safe in the garden and truly happy. Now I know Pam who is kindred in spirit and monetarily successful in building this type of landscape.

Closing my eyes, I thank my Higher Power. Now I know why I was asked to wait. It took a little longer than two weeks, but not much longer, to be gifted with another place to work. I suppose the Universe needs time to line things up. But I know now that God heard my prayers once again. My trust in Him is building along with trust in myself. When I do the right thing to take care of myself, doors open.

THE 187TH DAY

Today is my interview with Pam, and I arrive right on time. She came out of her home to great me, and we tour the property. I notice that she lives up to what she writes in the brochure. There is no sign of mowed grass and the garden is filled with native plants and old-fashioned red Monarda, Yarrow, Balloon Flowers, and Morning Glory. As we walked the wooded area of her property, Pam pointed out the four criteria that must be met in order to have a natural habitat. First is food, which consists of seed heads, berries, and birdseed; a water source such as a birdbath or pool; shelter, which can be a big pile of sticks and other debris and birdhouses, and a safe place for wildlife to raise their young.

In addition to being an active member of the local wildlife rescue organization, Pam takes care of feral cat colonies and three rescue dogs. Birds are singing everywhere, and grasses and pokeweed grow wild. She teaches that the more birds deliberately attracted to the property, the more non-beneficial insects will be eaten. Bats eat up to a thousand mosquitoes per hour. The key is keeping a natural balance in order to avoid using pesticides. The only fertilizer she uses is compost; feeding the soil with organic compost rather than synthetic fertilizers is the key to a healthy environment.

Not only are we kindred spirits, the job is also close to my house. The pay is far better than the nursery, and the season is longer. If I do not take this job, I need my head examined. We shake hands, and I think of Gert, Iris, Daisy and Rose. Smiling to myself, I remember that they've got along without me for many years, and they will continue for many more. Tomorrow I will put in my notice.

THE 230TH DAY

Everything up until this point has been about surviving, and now I need more balance in my life. I want to try something new. For many years, I still hold an interest in the paranormal and the questions of "life beyond". The world is full of magical surprise. After searching on the computer for a local paranormal investigation group, I came upon Gloria's group which is close to home for me. She and I meet at a local book store for an interview, and I am accepted to join them.

A few nights later, the group meets at a Potter's Field. The group members all seem committed and excited about possibly seeing an apparition or recording an E.V.P (electric voice phenomenon) to hear the actual spirit speak. Upon returning home, we all review our photos of energy orbs and some voices of spirits on our recorders. We email each other our evidence and made a date for another investigation.

Again, I am happy that I took another step to create an experience in my life. I could not be going ghost hunting if Seth were around. He had no interest in the paranormal, and there would be no time for me to join a group since Seth took up all of my free time. Meeting others on my own terms has been another empowering experience for me. The members seem to like me, and that affirms to me that I am 'loveable'. It feels good to laugh again and have fun.

Retiring to bed, I turn on the T.V. and witness an interview with a beautiful woman who had a narrow escape from an abusive boyfriend. After she broke off the relationship, he laid in wait at her home, and cornered her in her bedroom. He beat her beyond recognition. She said, "I got up off the floor to look at my face . . . . or what *used* to be my face. My nose was over on my cheek, and my eyes were red and bloodied. Blood had pooled below my head while I was lying on the carpet, and was filling my lungs. He had broken my cell phone, so I walked to my brother's house. He saw my face and his knees gave out. My boyfriend was arrested and they wanted to charge him with attempted murder. But I would not press the charges. In 30 days they let him out of jail. I went back together with him, as he promised he had changed. But then I soon saw the familiar evil in his eyes and the threat that it may happen again. I ended it with him, finally."

I turned off the T.V. and shuddered under the blankets. That could have been me. The beautiful girl could have been dead. Amazing how we go back to something that will kill us because we believe the empty promises. Again, I thanked God I am starting a new life.

THE 245ᵀᴴ DAY

Last year I had business cards of my own printed. The card advertises Labyrinths and meditation gardens along with traditional gardenscapes. Although I am still an inexperienced gardener, I have high hopes. My feeling is that we need to be *in* the garden, not just viewers on the sidelines. The garden is not a forbidden place that one can only admire from afar. In a garden, one is surrounded by a sacred space where there is wholeness and healing. Time seems to stop, and the moment is all that exists.

Two years ago, my friend Carol introduced me to Pastor Dorothy's church. Most of its members had died off or moved away, and it is struggling to stay afloat. I felt this would be a good place to build a labyrinth. A labyrinth is a meditation path built with sacred geometry design that is a tool to help the walker to go within and get in touch with the Divine and inner guidance. I spoke with Pastor Dorothy about this, and she felt it was a great idea. The time has come to start working on it.

After choosing the spot where I feel the labyrinth can be built, I just stare at the open lawn in complete fear of having misrepresented myself. Maybe I will completely deface the property! Although having traveled to visit other labyrinths and walked them, drawn them, and studied them, I was still far from having the courage to actually carve one into somebody's lawn. To make the job even more challenging, although the seven-circuit design is holy, I was tired of seeing the same design everywhere I went. I have decided to try something different.

Lying in bed, trying to sleep, I keep thinking about labyrinths. A spiral design comes to mind, but I dismiss that as being to easy. Relaxing my body, I pray for direction and let images appear in my mind's eye. The images floated in and out, and finally a flower design with seven petals settles into my inner-knowing space. The seven petals will represent the seven energy centers of the body and the Biblical number seven. A Seven Petal Labyrinth feels right. Starting to pay attention to the feelings in my solar plexus is something I never allowed myself to do before, as the truth felt too scary. Now, however, I welcome it.

THE 260TH DAY

Two weeks ago, I asked the landscape company not to cut the grass at the church so I could mow the labyrinth design into the growing lawn. Today I stand staring at the yard with divining rods in hand. Steve from the Lyceum taught me how to dowse. Pushing past the fear and using the rods, I dowse for where the center of the labyrinth should be and it's entrance. After marking these two areas with red flags a foot high I begin walking out the fifty-foot flower pattern, sticking flags in the ground as I go. After tracing the flower, I stand on the steps of the church and survey the flags, which look crazy and make no sense. Taking a deep breath, I shake the can of landscape paint, point it downward, and trace the flags.

The next task is the lawn mower. After taking another deep breath, I start the machine and trace the paint pattern as closely as possible with the mower. Once that sweaty task is complete, I stand on the church steps once again, and there is the seven petal flower! Skipping out onto the lawn and walking the pattern is being in heaven. I am *truly* happy!

The path textures will be made out of stone and other material. I've read that a meditation path needs different sounds underfoot to keep the walker in the moment. As I walk the grass path, however, I begin to understand that building this spiritual tool is the same process as my life choices. I am feeling the fear, and doing it anyway, and trusting God to lead. Just as I do not know my life plan in the end, I am uncertain of the labyrinth's final outcome. It is all on-going, and can be as beautiful as I make it.

One thing I know for sure . . . if I hadn't closed the door on Seth, this moment would not be happening. There would be no labyrinth, and there would be no "me" as I am today.

THE 265TH DAY

Since becoming single, interesting arrays of men have asked me out on a date. I have declined. In my codependence anonymous group, the opening paragraph reads, "The only requirement for membership is a desire for healthy and fulfilling relationships with ourselves and others." I note that the creed says "ourselves" before referring to relationships with others. I am just learning to have a healthy relationship with *me*, so I am not ready yet for the others.

I am realizing that I can be brave and creative and can choose healthier people to be in my life and do not have to put up with abuse from anyone.

Feeling good is starting to feel more normal than feeling rotten.

It would be lovely to have a glass of wine with a meal or a glass of brandy on a cold winter night, but only if I know how to stop after that one or two or three drinks. Otherwise, an alcohol related problem will bring me down into the pit of hell again. It is the same with relationships. It would be nice to have someone to share important moments—such as a beautiful view or an accomplishment—but, like drinking, the relationship would eventually turn into a nightmare.

Admitting that I have no idea how to have a grown-up relationship, it is relieving to know that it is perfectly fine to feel this way at this stage in my quest for self-knowledge. There is no "I *have* to" in my life right now. I can finally do what I want to do, and it is an exhilarating feeling. There is time—the rest of my natural life—to choose everything on my path.

THE 276ᵗʰ DAY

Working for Pam is rewarding so far. The work crew is enjoyable and they seem to like me. Thanks to Domingo and Pedro, my Spanish is becoming more proficient. New plant names are being added to my horticulture vocabulary. My confidence in gardening abilities is increasing.

It is late in the season, but the sun is still hot and the gardens are at their most magnificent peak. An amazing variety of birds have taken up residence at this particular estate and their combined song is from heaven. In a clearing at the far side of the property, I am having my lunch consisting of almond butter and jelly sandwich, and I am reminded of the botanical gardens Seth and I frequently visited.

Sitting alone at a stone table, I was suddenly struck by the absolute emptiness of the bench on the opposite side of the table. This moment is the first time I feel completely—internally—alone. The menacing bench just sits there . . . a lump of stone silence.

I think about all my "families". My blood family, work family, church family, paranormal family, twelve-step family, and my two dogs that all care for me. A feeling of inner warmth rises up and surrounds me. I feel abundantly blessed.

If I hadn't fostered my faith and belief in my ability to walk forward and holding God's hand the whole way, and let go of Seth, I never would have sat in this wonderful place and felt all these blessings.

THE 290TH DAY

"So then neither he who plants is anything, nor he who watered, but God who gives the increase."

(1 Corinthians 3:7)

The labyrinth is now sufficiently completed to be useable. For the whole summer season I spent every weekend working to remove the grass on the tips of the seven petals and to lay plastic over the design and place small stones on top to hide the plastic. Some of the paths have slate and stepping stones, while other sections have pieces of broken terracotta pots to walk on. A moat was built to be stepped across on larger stones and I combined the round cement pavers with inlaid glass to form mosaic designs that I built myself and would lie here and there on the paths. Other places are filled with planters, benches, and arbors. Maryann helped with sinking the Belgium blocks into the earth for the outline, and a grassy hill was built to challenge the walker to cross over on the journey to the center. The center of the labyrinth is adorned with pieces of finished marble.

Ida made a large banner from her recycled materials that read, "The Seven Petal Labyrinth is designed to depict life: simple and easy in the beginning, becoming more challenging and mindful in the middle, and then simple and easy toward the end as wisdom has been learned. The seven petals represent the seven energy centers of the body and the Biblical number seven. The stem of the flower is the start of the journey. Walking a labyrinth will put the walker in the present moment, which is where we connect to our Higher Power. God is not in the past or the future, but in the present moment. One can walk slowly and deliberately and be mindful of each step and each moment, or dance one's way through; combining our life energy with the labyrinth's natural life-force. The energy of the earth and heaven meet in the labyrinth. Either way one chooses to journey the labyrinth is the journey they need to take."

As I practice walking the labyrinth, I realize what a wonderful tool it is for coming to know oneself. It is a microcosm of a larger journey. How fast or slow do I walk? What am I thinking about while I am on the path? How is my body feeling? Am I experiencing the scene around me as negative or positive? I experience these things and much more as well as a presence of Spirit when I focus on connecting with that particular energy. We are all energy, and the environment around us is even more energy; all vibrating at different rates of speed. The more I walk the paths, the more jewels they bring forth.

This weekend is the Christening ceremony for the labyrinth. Seventy people attend. Among the many who respond to the invitation are Pam, Ida, my church family, my blood family, Carol, and a couple from my paranormal group. I am surrounded by so much love and joy! Steve came to help bless the center with Pastor Dorothy using holy water, and two drummers from South Africa came to play the instruments in the center of the labyrinth to "wake the Earth's life force". After walking the paths, everyone indulges in the lunch of chili that Maryann had prepared. At the end of the event, Pastor Dorothy suggested that I start giving workshops in the future and start a Labyrinth Ministry. It is a wonderful opportunity that I never would have considered in the past! More shall be revealed!

The 310th Day

A group home for the disabled had attended the labyrinth ceremony. One of the residents, a blind man, wanted to walk the path. Supported on either side by his two caregivers and his cane, he walked the entire flower. He was so happy with the experience which gave me the idea to build a labyrinth for the challenged. My brother, who was born with cerebral palsy, could also enjoy such an experience.

I discussed this idea with Pam, and I phoned a large organization for the disabled and spoke to the head C.E.O. named Paul. He was interested in the idea. After researching online for wheel-chair accessible material, I found a site specifically for gardens for the disabled. Ideas abounded with using scents and sounds for the blind, and raised beds for the wheel-chair bound.

Pam and I arrived for the meeting with Paul, and were seated at a long polished table with a group of business executives. What could have been an intimidating situation was made easy by my excitement about the presentation. Paul and his staff agreed to the project, and wanted raised beds, in the ground beds, and a labyrinth that was wide enough for wheel-chairs and walkers. Paul explained that he was raised on a farm, and had always dreamed of doing just what we were proposing, but had waited to find the right people to do the job.

Outside, after the meeting ended Pam and I high-five each other. We feel the project has offered us an even higher purpose for our organic gardens. Ideas come from Source. They are not solely mine. If I ignored my inner promptings and disregarded my heart and inner-voice, this garden may not have come into existence. It is a win-win-win situation; good for the organization, the clients, and our business. This is how relationships should be . . . everyone wins.

THE 319TH DAY

Maryann calls and invites me to the movies. I am eager to go. Sitting in the theater, the movie is about couples who emotionally drift apart over the years, but by the end of the movie they are falling in love with each other all over again. Thoughts of Seth come to mind. I long for him to tell me how he can't be without me and how he wants to make things right. I remember those moments when he would end up on my doorstep after having ended the relationship and being gone for quite some time. We would have that moment of reunion when we were lost in the feeling of love, falling into bed and making love for what seemed to be an eternity. We were lost in that wonderful place where there is no time except in that one moment. Then I remember how, within a week, the slow death-dance would surely follow. It happened time and time again, no matter how I tried to change the pattern; the dance had a life of its own.

Even though Seth wasn't good for me, maybe I wasn't good for him either. Sometimes I hear myself say aloud, "Please make him pay for what he's done to me!" But I just need to let things go. The priority now is that I be good to myself, the people I care about, and to the people who are yet to come into my life.

THE 336TH DAY

The temperature is freezing outside already and the earth is quieting for its winter sleep. The rhododendron leaves curl downward, and the birds are quiet. The sound of cars and trucks rumbling by on the street is louder now, as the fallen leaves of the trees no longer buffer the determined sound.

I am quiet, too. Images of Seth still come to mind at least once per day, but they are more as still photographs than film animations. Perhaps I am healing into a melancholy state rather than a constant, heavy sadness.

A few evenings ago, I learn that Seth is going to India again this winter. Without warning, the feelings of shock, rage and jealousy overwhelm me with the same intensity as when he first told me of these plans almost a year ago. I am still experiencing the "pang" of those feelings along with an emotional hangover and bad attitude toward the people closest to me. I suppose I need the people who care about me to understand the pain I am in, but that is not possible. This is my pain to deal with.

I turn my attention to my relationship with God, my plans for the future, and my growing relationship with myself. My eye wanders to a pillow in the corner of the couch where I am sitting. The pillow is made of at least a hundred tiny mirrors held together by yellow and black embroidery. I bring the pillow to my face, but I can't see my reflection, as the mirrors are small and cloudy. This is the equivalent of the process of spiritual growth. It takes time and effort, and a continual unfolding of soft, gentle revelations. By reflecting on this productive information, I begin to see my circumstances more clearly.

The hard work of growing up pays off with the lightness and relief that arrives after the pain and turmoil eventually lift. I am brought another step closer to inner freedom and the joy of living.

THE 337TH DAY

Seated at my upstairs window, I am watching evening approach. The sky is darkening and snow is blowing across the front yard and street as cars travel cautiously by. A couple walks by, bundled up so they both look like men. Everything is drawn in shades of gray as the first blizzard of the season approaches. Two major holidays are on their way that I need to navigate without my relationship with Seth.

Surprisingly, he sent me an email this morning. It read, "A warm and Merry Christmas to you. Would you like to go to the museum today in the storm? Or the ballet on Wednesday night? Or to India for eight weeks? Please let me know." Like a jerk, I responded by saying that I didn't have the money for India this year, just as a dig to remind him that he never helped out financially, although he practically lived in my home. The email returned to me marked "blocked". I suppose that is his way of having the last word.

Sadness returns. In the past, Seth would give me dates of an event way in advance, and I'd have to pray that life did not interfere with the plans. The mounting anxiety I would feel as the dates approached was a response to perhaps something unavoidable happening to thwart the plans, and the retaliation would be horrible. To this day, Seth still has no idea that his actions have anything to do with my ending the relationship.

I turn my attention back to the rapidly darkening evening and the approach of the storm and remind myself of why I left him and what my lessons are; where I would like my future to go, and who I am.

THE 339TH DAY

While standing in line at the supermarket, I see a magazine's headline that reads, "Give yourself a lift this season with a new bra, cool boots, and luscious lipsticks!" The message sounds enticing, but something doesn't feel right. No magazine ever says, "Give yourself a lift this season by helping feed the poor and rescuing abandon animals!" It seems that everywhere I look is an opportunity for a quick fix from buying something, sexing, drinking, drugging, and eating. After a brief high, they all leave us worse off than before we indulged. What is wrong with our society that it is so difficult to feel good? Is it being out of touch with God? Is it the food we eat or financial uncertainty? Is it because there is so much loss that we are in a constant state of grief? This is a question to which I still have no answer.

I am still practicing how to feel good in a self-loving, life-enhancing way. If we are perpetually helping others and not taking care of ourselves in the process, we can be left feeling drained and resentful. I am learning to walk the balance between self and others. Lately, I feel all I am doing is stringing a bunch of good days together with sadness in-between. A discolored and ugly necklace comes to mind.

I am not going to give up on moving forward and the prayer that life can be good . . . all the time. Even when tragedy strikes us, life can become good again. We need to find the lessons in the tragedy and use it positively. Otherwise, tragedy will become permanent scars on our hearts . . . closing the heart for years, if not forever.

THE 342ND DAY

"For the Kingdom of God is not in word, but in power.
What do you want? Shall I come to you with a rod, or in
love and a spirit of gentleness?"
(I Corinthians 4:20, 21)

I am wondering how Seth feels without me this holiday. Judging by last week's email, I guess there is a part of him that still can't believe I've really moved on.

As I am wrapping gifts this morning, I think about his gifts he gave to me last year. To his credit, all were useful to me and into which he put some thought. I bless last year's holiday and brought myself back to the present. I am filled with gratitude that I will not have to deal with the extra pressure of his demands and moods this year. The social itinerary he would have planned for us would have been exhausting and void of any of my requests or desires. Trying to keep the peace between my friends and family and Seth was always impossible, as no one wanted him around, and he also didn't want to be in their company.

While out shopping for gifts this afternoon, I pass by the display window of a card shop. On a shelf with a lot of other bric-a-brac is a small nativity scene with the word "Love" written on it. Before this journey began last year, the nativity scene would have been as cold in my heart as it would be to the touch; just a plastic decoration. But today, as I gazed at it, I felt my heart warm and fill with Love.

On that sidewalk, outside a cheap card shop in a strip mall, I am reminded that I am loved as a child of the Universe and by all the powers that be, and everyone on earth is loved just as much by the same power.

THE 345TH DAY

Another major holiday has come and gone without Seth with only one more to go. The experience of the passing holiday proved to be survivable, and I am looking forward to this year of mourning to be over. I have read that a person needs to go through a year of holidays and memories before a loss gets easier. Whether it will be easier remains to be seen, but I am hopeful.

Wondering what took me so long to break off such a potentially dangerous relationship, leads me to do more reading. I learn that on a first date, an abusive person doesn't reach across the table and punch you in the mouth. It is a subtle process that progresses into hell as time goes on. The first time the abuse occurs, it can be a shock when the real person pops out from behind the "nice mask". The victim is caught off balance, and can begin to doubt his or her own judgment. Then we can begin to think that the abuse must be our fault, since how could this wonderful individual with whom we are so in love possibly have had that type of terrible reaction if we hadn't provoked it in some way?

Most victims end up in this weird place of knowing they should get out, but the abuse cycle is like being caught on a carnival ride that won't stop to let us off. When my son was little I took him on a Ferris wheel ride. Squirming on my lap, trying to be free to move around and look over the side of the cart at the lights below, I held on to him tighter. The more I held on to him, the more he squirmed. Panic-stricken, I prayed each time we neared the ground that the wheel would stop and let us out, but it kept on going back up into the sky. The abusive relationship is very much the same. We pray that "this time" will be the last time, and that our beloved will "see the errors of his ways" and life will become happy again. However, unless there is a strong intervention of some kind the chance of change is next to nothing. Even with therapy and the threat of jail, abusers rarely change at their core. Usually a character disorder can be involved that makes change particularly difficult. My own narcissistic issues lead me to believe I could change someone. It is up to the person and God to perform that miracle.

If we live to get out of the mess, we begin to pick up the pieces of the shattered life that lies all around us. It is no good if we try to put it all back together again, as then the negative pattern just continues. We must sweep the pieces into the garbage and begin the long process of finding our own truths. We can do this by acts of loving kindness to ourselves that will rebuild self-esteem, and by acts of kindness to people who are receptive to them and who will love us back. In this way, we are less likely to end up in another abusive situation, as our self-love won't tolerate us being there.

THE 351ST DAY

The last major holiday of the year has passed without Seth. It is literally a new year, full of promise. Over the last three days I am revamping my life by cleaning out the two upstairs rooms. I bag up and throw out hundreds of pounds of dead clutter that stands as a reminder of my years with Seth. I even throw out furniture that no longer serves any useful purpose. My emotional "junk" allowed me to become buried under physical junk from depression and procrastination. Now that I have rid myself of the physical clutter, I already have more lightness of being. My home is my sanctuary, and I want to feel good when I walk in the door.

Now that Seth is gone physically and emotionally, I can peel back more layers of the metaphysical onion and see what issues I own by myself that have nothing to do with Seth.

Procrastination is a self-fulfilling prophesy. The more I procrastinate, the more overwhelmed I feel and the more anxiety and fear build up until I am completely immobilized. I am sure everyone puts things off from time to time, but in my case, procrastination is coming not only from a place of emotional immaturity, but from unrealistic fears of success and failure; fear of responsibility. When children are given either too much responsibility or not enough, issues arise related to understanding the proper way to take care of ourselves.

Although I have accomplished a great deal by letting go of things that aren't good for me and replacing the space with inspiring endeavors, I still wasn't being kind to myself on a daily basis. I saw another magazine headline today that read, "Are you loving yourself today?" The answer was usually "no", as I am always doing something out of survival rather than self-love. After a few days of de-cluttering the two rooms, and the job is done for now, I go downstairs to make some pancakes. Not because I have to, but because I want to. I prepare them with all the finest organic ingredients, put them on a pretty plate, and eat them. True peace and contentment fill me during and after this process. This simple act gave me a "taste" of what it feels like to be loving to myself. Now, I can pass this love on to someone else because I genuinely have it to give.

THE 353RD DAY

After coming home from this evening's Taize service, I sit down to reflect on the evening. The Christian service includes meditation, candle-lighting, reading from the gospel, and chant songs in Latin. The music director was late, so the chorus of five singers was off key, the piano player didn't play well, and Elizabeth from South Africa really put her "groove on". The whole scene was so badly done that we all had to laugh. After service we all had a good time eating healthy food and walking the indoor labyrinth rug. If the church had to close its doors because of lack of funds, I will so miss the support and opportunities for growth I've experienced here.

I read in a Christian magazine that only the spirit is real and matter is "false". The article confirms what I have been learning all through this journey. Objects that we see are nothing more than molecules of different densities that come together to form things that will eventually break down and fade away. Matter is just here to embody spirit. Everything has an aura of vibrational frequency and we are all connected. My energy intertwines with other people's energy and the environment's energy, and the environment's energy affects my energy. We are all connected on this planet and beyond.

Down the coastline from where I live is a public observatory with a huge telescope. I plan to visit there with my dad for his birthday. I want to see Jupiter and Mars, the beautiful galaxies, and the nebulas, which are the "star nurseries" where stars are born. Since we are all microcosms of the bigger universe, I want to see and feel that connection to life here and beyond into the stars.

As I was cleaning up after Taize, I approach the altar to blow out the candles that each of us had lit in prayer during the service. Our dreams, hopes, pain, and gratitude are all lit up and held within that tray of candlelight that dances up and down against the darkened alter.

THE 356ᵀᴴ DAY

Sitting in church with my son today, I am aware of a feeling of emptiness; a total lack of enthusiasm today about everything. Why I feel this way eludes me, and it is disappointing to feel so lacking after all the work I've done. However, I have learned to "just be" with a feeling and see where it leads me. I think about the parishioners and some of their personal stories, and realize just how vulnerable we all are. My internal focus shifts to thoughts of God, and I wonder how I got along without making him my central focus.

How hard it is to change my way of thinking and to stop procrastinating, sabotaging and being attracted to miserable situations? I can't believe that I ever thought I had the power to change anyone else! Recovery has taught me that I do not have the power to change my character defects. All I need is the willingness to change and let go of what is not benefiting me, and God will do the rest.

One of the readings in my daily affirmation book this morning was about "doing the same thing over and over and expecting different results", which some consider the definition of insanity. Today, I am doing things differently, and the results are rewarding. The universe hates a void, and somewhere during this day, my emptiness will be filled with something else. I can choose what that will be.

THE 365TH DAY

"Let a man so consider us, as servants of Christ and
stewards of the mysteries of God."

(1 Corinthians 4:1)

The Last Night

This is the last twenty-four hours of my year's journey into healing.
Although this is the last night, it is just a new beginning.

Today is Ida's 24th sober anniversary celebration. Standing in the front of
a room filled with supporters are Ida and three other women celebrating
their own sober anniversaries. Each woman is as radiant and beautiful as
the next. Their stories of the pain of drinking, the pain of early sobriety,
and then the rewards and joy of living are intensely inspiring. One of the
women brought in a bag of tiny mustard seeds and she passes them around
to the supporters. She speaks about being told, when in early sobriety, that
all a person needs to succeed is faith the size of a mustard seed. I have
found this to be true. Faith the size of a mighty tree comes from that first
seed.

After the meeting is over, I take the five minute drive to the ocean. Although
I live only three miles from the Atlantic, I never seem to take advantage of
it by going to the beach. My solace has always been found in the woods
and fields rather than the ocean. As I walk up the dunes, I am met by
the sight of beautiful, white winter weeds growing generously within the
beach grass. The sun glows from behind the opaque winter clouds, and
the waves brake close to the shoreline. The wind blows a steady whistle
against my ears, while the smell of seaweed and salt water fill my senses.

The power of Mother Nature is everywhere. Looking up at the sun and
speaking aloud, I thank my Creator for my life and for everyone in it.
I thank him for the past, present, future, and the energizing peace and
gratitude I feel on so many levels, and for the knowledge that everything
is always going to be survivable.

An email that my aunt sent me comes to mind. She told a story about visiting a Pacific coast beach in California named Point Dume. While walking down the beach searching for shells and beach glass, she looked up to see a whale emerge from the water. Soon, a cluster of dolphins also surfaced to swim alongside the whale. My aunt was alone on the beach and was totally taken in by the moment. Although such a wonderful sight would never appear on my Atlantic beach, I can guess that the feeling of awe, gratitude, and the sense of God's presence were the same for my aunt as they are for me today.

Tonight I am driving to another town to meet with my ghost hunting buddies at a diner for snacks. Other groups will be joining us, and I will have another opportunity to meet new people and have a good time. My son is leaving for a weekend of snowboarding where he, too, will have a good time. Life is good today. Whatever life brings me this coming year, I will walk through it and learn and grow. In my constant quest for love, I have found it. It is . . . everywhere!

Exercise Gifts with Love (1 Corinthians: 13: 1-13)

Though I speak with the tongues of men
and angels, but have not love, I have
become sounding brass or clanging cymbal.

And though I have the gift of prophecy,
and understand all mysteries and knowledge,
and though I have all faith, so that I
could remove mountains, but have not love,
I am nothing.

And though I bestow all my goods to
feed the poor, and though I give my body to
be burned, but have not love, it profits me
nothing.

Love suffers long and is kind; love
does not envy; love does not parade itself, is
not puffed up;

Does not behave rudely, does not seek
its own, is not provoked, thinks no evil;

Does not rejoice in iniquity, but rejoices
in truth;

bears all things, believes all things,
hopes all things, endures all things.

Love never fails. But whether there are
prophecies, they will fail; whether there are
tongues, they will cease; whether there is
knowledge, it will vanish away.

For we know in part and we prophesy in part
but when that which is perfect has come,
then that which is in part will be done away.

When I was a child, I spoke as a child. I
understood as a child, I thought as a child;
but when I became a man, I put away childish things.

For now we see in a mirror, dimly, but then face to face.
Now I know in part,
but then I shall know just as I also am known.
And now abide faith, hope love, these three; but the greatest of these
Is love.

Afterword Revised

"As the garden grows, so does the gardener."
—Anonymous

As we grow, the Corinthians prayer takes on a deeper meaning, and different verses become significant. When the prayer refers to love-energy as being patient and kind and suffering, it is definitely not referring to being abused. God did not create us in his perfect image for us to buy into being put down and shut up or perhaps killed. We can let go with love, and move along to help ourselves and others who appreciate us.

The word "Macantar" is a Gaelic word meaning kindness, meekness; honesty. If the word is "Macanta", the meaning is excellence, gentle, modest, childlike, decent, and honorable. Yet another definition means to "transform into our original essence." These words are the ingredients to lead a decent life, providing healthy boundaries are in place. They allow us to become open to change and to have the humility needed for a higher power to guide us. In this way, we can learn to build our strength of character and the courage we need to keep moving forward.

Just as standing inside the garden is far more magical than just looking at it from beyond its borders, so is the idea of being inside these words and living them rather than contemplating the words from a distance.

Three years have passed since I wrote these entries and some people are no longer with me. Carol passed from a major stroke. She lingered for a week in the hospital, and upon removing life-support, she slowly died. Steve from the Lyceum passed a month later from a massive heart attack in a parking lot after a beekeeping class. We knew his health was failing, but did not expect this sudden departure. These two deaths happened within a month's time of each other, and have left major holes in our community of friends. Carol and Steve were the salt of the earth. My job with Pam came to a sad ending also, as I didn't use my discernment skills about what may be coming down the road with her, and my idealism blinded my common sense. Our beloved church may be closing this spring due to lack of funds, and I will mourn the loss of all those wonderful times of learning, growing and the labyrinth. During my Macantar story, I chose the changes I needed to make, but now the Universe is picking the changes, and I need to accept and adapt. I no longer feel like a victim when circumstances lead to "negative" outcomes. Instead, I need to look at my part in the play of life, and change what I can and have the wisdom to know the things that I can't change, as the serenity prayer says.

Instead of pushing away the pain or loss, I need to embrace and love it. It is the only way to transform anything. I watch as my beloved pets are producing grey fur, I am turning grey, and I am taking my parents to the appropriate places for end of life planning. My son is speaking of marriage. This is life . . . the never ending cycle of ebb and flow.

Once again, I am standing in a place of uncertainty for my future. But I only need to deal with today. I can put in the footwork to pave a way to a good life, but I cannot control the outcome. Carol and I had a discussion shortly before her death that a leaf cannot will itself to stay green on the branch forever. There are laws of beginnings and endings, and then another beginning. When the moon becomes full, and wants to wane, we can look at that moment as a new beginning rather than a prelude to an end. Spirit is in charge, and I will see my path if I just stay open and listen for guidance.

Being without a significant other for this much time has been challenging and tremendously good for me. I now look for support in healthier and life-giving places. Maybe someday, I will be open to a relationship, but for now I am still learning the lessons of being solo. I have found the holy to be in places other than couple relationships. My friend Valarie Griggs says it all in one of her songs:

I left the worn path for settling down
for deserts and forests
to see how the holy is hiding
all around.

And I met the poets in love with the Spirit
tireless pilgrims singing the body electric (A Walt Whitman Allusion)

And I love so much and so well
without having found the love of my life!

BIBLIOGRAPHY

Griggs, Valerie. Around the Far Turn. Cosmic Funnybone Records 2007, compact disc.

Bancroft, Lundy. Why Does He Do That? Inside the Minds of Angry and Controlling Men. Berkley Books (Sept. 2, 2003).

Tomkins, Peter. The Secret Life of Plants. Harper and Row (March 8, 1989).

The Findhorn Community. The Findhorn Garden: Pioneering a New Vision of Man and Nature in Cooperation. Harper Collins (1976).